The Burden of Comfort:

Escapism, Purpose, and the Quest for True Rest

"If you come seeking what you expect to find, this book will not offer it.
If you seek only confirmation, you will walk away with nothing.
But if you seek awareness, the beginning of seeing will unfold.
You choose whether to walk this path — or remain where you are."

Copyright

The Burden of Comfort (eBook Edition)

The Burden of Comfort

© 2026 Conde Cagalitan

All rights reserved.

No part of this publication may be reproduced, stored in a retrieval system, or transmitted in any form or by any means—electronic, mechanical, photocopying, recording, or otherwise—without prior written permission from the author, except in the case of brief quotations used in reviews, scholarly work, or critical analysis.

This book is a work of original philosophy. Any resemblance to actual persons, living or dead, is coincidental. The reflections and arguments herein represent the author's contemplative inquiry into the psychological, cultural, and existential forces shaping the modern human condition.

Published by Conde D. Cagalitan

eBook Edition

ISBN: 979-8-2491-0058

Cover design and interior design by Conde Cagalitan

The Author's Canon

Ceremonial Introduction

These works form a single unfolding journey — a canon built to guide the reader from myth to meaning, and from meaning to coherence.

Each volume is a threshold, each threshold a movement deeper into the architecture of awakening.

A Sequential Guide to the Mythic and Philosophical Works.

Mythic Wing — Narrative Foundations

Stories that awaken the symbolic imagination and prepare the heart for truth.

The Dawn That Knows Your Name — Trilogy

The Last Human

Philosophical Wing — The Foundational Framework

Works that articulate the metaphysical, psychological, and existential structure of the human journey.

God Beyond Existence

The Burden of Comfort

The Unbreakable Rules

Future volumes in the unfolding philosophical architecture

Acknowledgments

There are journeys we walk with others, and journeys we walk alone.
This book was both.

To those who have walked beside me — in conversation, in silence, in prayer, or in simple presence — thank you. Your honesty, your questions, and your own struggles with distraction and purpose helped shape the heart of this work.

To the people who shared their stories of weariness, escape, and longing for rest — your vulnerability reminded me that this burden is universal, and that the call to return is for all of us.

To the teachers, pastors, and thinkers who helped form my understanding of Scripture and the human condition — your wisdom echoes through these pages.

To my family and loved ones — thank you for your patience, your encouragement, and your quiet strength. You have been a living reminder of grace.

And above all, to the One who never stopped calling me back from the noise —
thank You for rest, for purpose, and for the gentle yoke that makes life whole again.

Dedication

For every soul who has ever escaped into comfort
because reality felt too heavy.
You are seen.
You are loved.
You are called home.

The Metanarrative

Every book is born from a story larger than itself.
This work began as a reflection on escapism, but it belongs to a deeper journey — a quiet exploration of the human condition, the ache beneath modern comfort, and the ancient call to return to the One who gives true rest.
It is the first movement in a broader vision:
a path from disorientation to awakening,
from fragmentation to wholeness,
from comfort to purpose.
You do not need to see the whole journey now.
It is enough to take the first step.
This version is:

- subtle
- philosophical
- poetic
- canon-aware without being explicit
- perfectly suited to sit between the Dedication and the Preface

Table of Contents

The Author's Canon i
Acknowledgments ii
Dedication iii
The Metanarrative iv
Preface: The Agony of the Band-Aid 1
PART I — THE DIAGNOSIS: WHY WE ESCAPE 3
    Chapter 1: The Band-Aid Remedy 4
    Chapter 2: The Divine vs. the Distraction 6
    Chapter 3: The Problem of Gloom and Unfairness ... 8
    Chapter 4: The Blueprint of Glory 10
PART II — THE ORIGIN: THE GLORY AND THE FALL 12
    Chapter 5: The Rebellion and the Corrupted Heart 13
    Chapter 6: The Failure of Human Effort 15
PART III — THE SOLUTION: THE UNMERITED GIFT 17
    Chapter 7: The Promise of the Crusher 18
    Chapter 8: The Divine Substitute 20
PART IV — THE TRUE REST: A LIFE OF PURPOSE 21
    Chapter 9: The Yoke Made Easy 22
    Chapter 10: The Active Defense Against Distraction 24
    Epilogue: Come Unto Me 26
    Conclusion: The End of Escape, the Beginning of Life 27
    Reflection & Next Steps: Walking in True Rest 30
    Final Encouragement About the Author 34
    About the Author 36

The Canon Continues 37

Preface: The Agony of the Band-Aid

This book did not begin as a sermon. It began as a shared observation about a universal human struggle: the desperate need to escape.

Every one of us knows the weight of the "gloomy situation"—the quiet ache of personal failure, the injustice of the world, the heaviness of unanswered questions, and the persistent disquiet of the soul. And when that weight becomes too much, we reach for comfort. We scroll. We binge. We numb. We run.

This response is understandable. It is human. But what if the comfort we seek is not healing us at all?
What if it is only making us comfortable in our captivity?

Temporary relief—whether through entertainment, distraction, or emotional numbing—does not mend the wound. It simply covers it. It is a band-aid placed over a spiritual fracture. And when distraction becomes the norm, it reshapes our lives into something passive and hollow. We become, in our own words, "prisoners waiting for final judgment"—not only God's judgment, but the judgment of a life unlived and a purpose abandoned.

Over time, I came to see escapism not merely as a psychological habit, but as a spiritual resistance. It is the human heart clinging to the oldest lie in Eden: *"You can be god. You can steer your own ship."*
And so we hide—not in fig leaves this time, but in screens, noise, and endless entertainment.

This book is an exploration of the antidote.
We do not condemn rest, joy, or the simple pleasures of art. These are gifts. But we confront the deeper truth: that the ultimate answer to human pain is not found in escape, but in purpose. Not in distraction, but in devotion. Not in self-reliance, but in surrender.

Our journey moves from the original Divine Purpose to the Fall, through the burden of the Law, and finally to the lightness of Grace found in Christ. It is a journey from the heavy burden of comfort to the easy, purposeful yoke of the Redeemer.

This book is an invitation—
to stop running,
to stop numbing,
to stop hiding,
and to return.

True rest is not found in fleeing life, but in giving it back to the One who made it.

PART I — THE DIAGNOSIS: WHY WE ESCAPE

Chapter 1: The Band-Aid Remedy

Every human heart carries wounds. Some are fresh and obvious; others are buried beneath years of silence. But all of us, at some point, feel the weight of life pressing down—failure, disappointment, injustice, loneliness, fear, guilt, or the quiet ache of meaninglessness.

And when the weight becomes too much, we reach for relief.

Entertainment becomes the easiest band-aid. A show, a game, a scroll, a song—anything that can numb the ache for a moment. It works just long enough to make us forget the wound, but never long enough to heal it.

This is the tragedy of escapism:
it comforts us while quietly deepening our captivity.

We begin to live for the next distraction. We avoid the hard questions. We silence the inner cry. We trade the discomfort of growth for the comfort of avoidance. And slowly, without noticing, we become prisoners of our own coping mechanisms.

But escapism is not the disease.
It is the symptom.

Behind every escape is a deeper spiritual wound—a longing for meaning, justice, rest, and purpose that entertainment cannot satisfy. The band-aid covers the pain, but the infection remains.

This chapter names the wound.
The next chapters reveal its source.

Chapter 2: The Divine vs. the Distraction

Every worldview—religious or secular—recognizes the tension between the temporary comforts of the world and the deeper call of the soul. But the Christian tradition frames this tension with particular clarity:

God is the ultimate answer to the human dilemma.
Distraction is the counterfeit.

Entertainment is not evil in itself. But when it becomes the primary refuge of the heart, it becomes a spiritual competitor. It absorbs the time, attention, and affection that were meant for God.

This is why Scripture warns repeatedly about the danger of "worldly distractions."
Not because joy is sinful,
but because misplaced devotion is.

Across traditions:

Christianity warns against idolatry and wasted purpose.
Islam warns against dunya (the worldly life) overshadowing akhira (the eternal life).
Buddhism warns against attachment and craving.
Judaism warns against frivolity that steals time from holiness and study.

Different languages.
Different metaphors.
Same human struggle.

The heart is easily captivated by what is easy, immediate,

and pleasurable.

But the soul is only healed by what is eternal.

This chapter exposes the spiritual dimension of distraction.

The next chapter confronts the question that drives it.

Chapter 3: The Problem of Gloom and Unfairness

Here we reach the heart of the struggle.
If God is good, why is the world so full of suffering?
If God is just, why does injustice flourish?
If God is powerful, why does evil persist?

This is the question that haunts believers and skeptics alike.

It is the question that drives people toward escapism.
It is the question that makes comfort so tempting.

When the world feels unfair, the soul seeks refuge.
When life feels heavy, the heart seeks escape.
When suffering feels senseless, distraction feels justified.

But the problem of suffering is not merely emotional — it is theological.

The Christian answer begins not with human pain, but with divine purpose.

Scripture teaches that God's thoughts are not our thoughts, and His ways are not our ways.

Creation is not centered on human comfort, but on God's glory.

And this world — broken as it is — is the stage upon which His justice, mercy, patience, and redemption are revealed.

This does not make suffering easy.
But it makes suffering meaningful.
The question "Why is life unfair?" cannot be answered until we first ask,

"Why did God create the world at all?"

Chapter 4: The Blueprint of Glory

Before we can understand the brokenness of the world, we must understand its original design. The story of humanity does not begin with suffering, injustice, or escapism. It begins with glory.

Creation was not an accident. It was a deliberate act of divine intention.

Time, space, and the physical world were crafted as the stage upon which God would reveal His character, His creativity, and His love.

Humanity was placed at the center of this design.

We were created not as spectators, but as partners — bearers of God's image, entrusted with stewardship, creativity, responsibility, and purpose. The physical world was a gift, a home, and a mission field. Every sunrise, every breath, every moment was meant to reflect the goodness and glory of the Creator.

In this original blueprint:
Work was meaningful.
Relationships were whole.
Purpose was clear.
Rest was natural.
God was near.

There was no need for escapism because there was nothing to escape from.

But something happened that shattered this harmony — something that explains the "gloomy situation" we now live in.

PART II — THE ORIGIN: THE GLORY AND THE FALL

Chapter 5: The Rebellion and the Corrupted Heart

The story of suffering does not begin on Earth.
It begins in Heaven.

Long before humanity fell, another being fell — Lucifer, the shining one, who desired the throne of God. His rebellion was rooted in pride, autonomy, and the desire to be his own master. When he was cast down, his mission became clear: corrupt the crown of God's creation.

And he succeeded.

The serpent's temptation in Eden was not about fruit. It was about identity.
It was the same lie he believed:

"You can be god. You can define good and evil. You can rule yourself."

When humanity accepted this lie, something catastrophic happened:
the heart was corrupted
the relationship with God was severed
the world was fractured
suffering entered the story
death became inevitable
the human will turned inward

The "gloom" we feel today is not random.
It is the echo of Eden's rebellion.

The human heart — once aligned with God — became bent toward self-rule.
And a heart bent inward cannot find rest.
This is why escapism feels so natural.

It is the heart trying to soothe a wound it cannot heal.

Chapter 6: The Failure of Human Effort

After the Fall, humanity tried to fix itself.

We built civilizations, laws, religions, philosophies, and moral systems. We tried to be good, to be strong, to be righteous, to be whole. But every attempt revealed the same truth:

The problem is not outside us.
The problem is within us.

The Law — given through Moses — was not a ladder to climb back to God.

It was a mirror, revealing the depth of our brokenness.

It showed that:

sin is not just an action
sin is a condition
sin is the default posture of the human heart

The Law proved that humanity cannot save itself.

We cannot heal our own wounds.
We cannot escape our own corruption.
We cannot carry the burden of our own guilt.

The spiritual burden is too heavy for human strength. This is why escapism feels so appealing — it offers temporary relief from a weight we were never meant to carry alone.

But the story does not end with failure.
The Law was not the cure — it was the diagnosis.

The cure was coming.

Part III reveals it.

PART III — THE SOLUTION: THE UNMERITED GIFT

Chapter 7: The Promise of the Crusher

The story of redemption begins long before Bethlehem. It begins in the garden where humanity fell.

The moment sin entered the world, God did not retreat. He did not abandon His creation. He did not leave humanity to drown in the consequences of its rebellion. Instead, He spoke a promise.

In Genesis 3:15 — often called the *Protoevangelium*, the first gospel — God declared that a Deliverer would come. A Child. A Seed. One who would crush the serpent's head and undo the devastation of the Fall.

This promise became the thread that runs through the entire Old Testament:

whispered to Abraham
preserved through Israel
foreshadowed in the sacrifices
proclaimed by the prophets
anticipated by generations

Every covenant, every law, every prophet, every story pointed forward to the One who would restore what was lost.

Humanity could not climb back to God.
So God promised to come down to humanity.

This chapter reveals the hope that suffering cannot erase: God Himself initiated the rescue.

Chapter 8: The Divine Substitute

The promise of the Crusher finds its fulfillment in the most astonishing act in history:

God became man. Not a prophet. Not a messenger. Not a moral teacher. But God Himself — entering the world He created, taking on flesh, stepping into the brokenness we caused. Why?

Because no human being was worthy.
No human effort was sufficient.
No human righteousness could bridge the gap.

The Law had already proven that humanity could not save itself.

So God provided the only solution that could work: A perfect Substitute.

Jesus Christ lived the life we could not live and died the death we could not bear.

He carried the weight of sin — the guilt, the shame, the judgment — so that we would not have to.

Grace is not God lowering the standard.
Grace is God meeting the standard on our behalf.

This is why salvation is a gift.

PART IV — THE TRUE REST: A LIFE OF PURPOSE

Chapter 9: The Yoke Made Easy

After the long journey through suffering, rebellion, and redemption, Jesus offers a simple invitation:

"Come to Me… and I will give you rest."

Not escape.
Not distraction.
Not temporary relief.

Rest.

True rest is not the absence of responsibility — it is the presence of purpose. It is the soul returning to its rightful center.

Jesus summarizes the entire human calling in two commands:

Love God with all your heart, mind, and soul.
Love your neighbour as yourself.

These are not burdens.
They are the natural expression of a heart aligned with God.

Love is the framework for human flourishing.
It is the antidote to escapism because love requires presence, attention, and engagement.

You cannot love while hiding.
You cannot love while numbing.

You cannot love while escaping.

The Holy Spirit empowers this love — not as a duty, but as a desire.

The believer is not forced into purpose; he is transformed into it.

This is the easy yoke: a life carried by grace, directed by love, and sustained by the Spirit.

Chapter 10: The Active Defense Against Distraction

The Christian life is not passive.
It is not a waiting room for heaven.
It is a commission.

Jesus' final command — "Go and make disciples of all nations" — is not a suggestion.

It is the believer's mission, identity, and calling.

Escapism collapses under the weight of this calling.

You cannot fulfill the Great Commission while living in retreat.
You cannot serve while numbing.
You cannot witness while hiding.

The New Covenant gives the believer:

the power of the Holy Spirit
the authority of Christ
the presence of God
the purpose of the Kingdom

This is the active defense against distraction:
a life so full of meaning that escapism loses its appeal.

Purpose is the cure for passivity.
Engagement is the cure for avoidance.
Service is the cure for self-absorption.

The believer is called to live in the real world —
to love, to serve, to witness, to build, to restore.

This is the life that defeats escapism.
This is the life that glorifies God.

Epilogue: Come Unto Me

At the end of all arguments, doctrines, and explanations, Jesus' invitation remains simple:

"Come unto Me… and I will give you rest."

The world offers comfort that numbs.
Christ offers rest that heals.

The world offers escape that delays.
Christ offers purpose that transforms.

The world offers distraction that drains.
Christ offers love that restores.

The heavy burden of self-reliance is replaced with the light burden of grace.

The restless heart finds its home.
The weary soul finds its peace.
The distracted mind finds its focus.

True rest is not found in running away from life,
but in surrendering life to the One who created it.

This is the end of escapism.
This is the beginning of purpose.
This is the rest your soul was made for.

Conclusion: The End of Escape, the Beginning of Life

Every journey has a turning point — a moment when the traveller realizes that the path ahead is no longer about running from something, but running toward something.

This book has traced the arc of that turning point.

We began with the ache of the human heart — the wounds, the disappointments, the injustices, the quiet despair that drives us toward distraction. We named escapism for what it is: a temporary comfort that numbs but never heals, a band-aid placed over a spiritual fracture.

We then followed the story back to its beginning — to the glory of creation, the tragedy of rebellion, and the corruption of the human heart. We saw that the "gloomy situation" of the world is not a contradiction of God's goodness, but the inevitable result of humanity's attempt to rule itself.

And yet, even in our rebellion, God did not abandon us. He pursued us.

Through promise, covenant, prophecy, and finally incarnation, God revealed the cure for the wound we could not heal. In Christ, the burden of guilt is lifted, the burden of performance is removed, and the burden of self-reliance is replaced with the easy yoke of grace.

This is the turning point.
This is where escape ends and life begins.

True rest is not found in avoiding reality, but in embracing the One who holds reality together.
True purpose is not found in self-creation, but in surrender to the One who created us.
True freedom is not found in autonomy, but in love — the love of God that transforms the heart and the love of neighbour that transforms the world.

The believer's life is not a retreat from the world, but a return to it.
Not as a prisoner of distraction, but as a witness of grace.
Not as a consumer of comfort, but as a bearer of purpose.
Not as one who hides, but as one who serves.

The world will always offer escape.
Christ will always offer rest.

The world will always offer distraction.
Christ will always offer purpose.

The world will always offer noise.
Christ will always offer peace.

The choice is not between entertainment and misery.
It is between temporary comfort and eternal rest.
Between numbing the wound and healing it.
Between living half-awake and living fully alive.

This book has been an invitation —
to stop running,
to stop numbing,
to stop hiding,
and to return.

Return to purpose.
Return to presence.
Return to love.
Return to Christ.

For in Him, the weary find rest,
the restless find peace,
and the wounded find healing.

This is the end of escapism.
This is the beginning of life.

Reflection & Next Steps: Walking in True Rest

Escapism loses its power when the soul becomes awake, anchored, and engaged.

This final section offers simple, practical steps to help you live the life this book has pointed toward — a life of purpose, presence, and true rest in Christ.

These are not rules.
They are invitations.
They are ways of returning to the One who calls you to rest.

Each practice is a small turning of the heart — a way of loosening the grip of escapism and learning to live awake, present, and rooted in God. None of them demand perfection. They simply open space for grace to work.

Heart Check: Three Daily Questions

At the end of each day, pause and ask:
1. What did I run from today?

Was it a feeling, a responsibility, a conversation, a truth, or a wound?

2. What did I run to?
Was it God, or was it distraction?
What is God inviting me to face with Him tomorrow?

Courage grows when we name what we fear.

These questions gently expose the patterns of avoidance and open the door to healing.

2. The Practice of Presence

Escapism thrives on fragmentation — a scattered mind, a restless heart, a distracted life.
Presence is the antidote.

Try this simple daily practice:
The 5-Minute Stillness

Sit in silence for five minutes.
No phone.
No music.
No agenda.
Just breathe and say, "Here I am, Lord."

This small act retrains the heart to return to God instead of running from itself.

3. The Discipline of Attention

Your attention is your most valuable spiritual resource.
Where your attention goes, your life follows.

Choose one of these each day:
Read a short passage of Scripture slowly.
Pray for one person with intention.
Notice one moment of beauty in your day.
Do one act of kindness without being seen.

These small practices reorient the heart toward love and purpose.

4. The Weekly Digital Sabbath

Once a week, choose a window of time — one hour,
three hours, or a full day — to step away from:
social media
streaming
gaming
endless scrolling
digital noise

Not as punishment.
As liberation.

Use that time to:
walk
pray
journal
talk with someone you love
rest
reflect
breathe

This rhythm breaks the cycle of dependency and restores
clarity.

5. The Courage to Engage

Escapism collapses when purpose rises.
Each week, choose one meaningful action:
serve someone in need
encourage a friend
volunteer
share your faith
reconcile a relationship

create something
help someone quietly

Purpose is not found in grand gestures.
It is found in small acts of love done consistently.

6. The Return to Christ

Above all, remember this:
You are not fighting escapism alone.

You are not healing your wounds alone.
You are not carrying your burdens alone.

Christ is not calling you to try harder.
He is calling you to come closer.

Return to Him daily — in weakness, in honesty, in surrender.

He is gentle.
He is patient.
He is rest.

Final Encouragement About the Author

You do not need to escape your life.

You need to rediscover the One who walks with you through it.

You do not need to numb your wounds.

You need the Healer who carries them.

You do not need to run from your purpose.

You need the Spirit who empowers it.

The burden of comfort is heavy.
The yoke of Christ is light.

Choose the light burden.
Choose the easy yoke.
Choose the rest your soul was made for.

About the Author

Conde D. Cagalitan is a Christian writer whose work explores the intersection of faith, purpose, and the human condition. With a voice shaped by philosophical reflection and a deep concern for the spiritual restlessness of modern life, he writes to awaken readers to the quiet call of God beneath the noise of distraction.

His work blends theology, existential insight, and pastoral clarity, guiding others toward inner transformation and a life anchored in love, presence, and devotion.

The Burden of Comfort is part of his broader vision to help individuals rediscover meaning, confront escapism, and return to the One who calls them home.

Conde lives in Australia, where he continues to write, reflect, and pursue the lifelong journey of spiritual renewal.

The Canon Continues

A Journey from Awakening to Understanding

The works of Conde D. Cagalitan form a unified canon — a mythic and philosophical architecture designed to guide the reader from symbolic intuition to metaphysical clarity, and from clarity to coherence.

Each volume stands alone, yet each belongs to a larger unfolding.

Mythic Wing — Narrative Foundations

Stories that awaken the inner landscape and prepare the heart for truth.

The Dawn That Knows Your Name — Trilogy

A journey from illusion to awakening, from fracture to calling.

The Last Human

A solitary witness in a world forgetting its soul.

Philosophical Wing — The Foundational Framework

Works that articulate the metaphysical, existential, and spiritual structure of the human condition.

God Beyond Existence

A comparative exploration of ultimate reality and the ground of all being.

The Burden of Comfort

A diagnosis of escapism and a call to return to purpose and true rest.

The Unbreakable Rules

A forthcoming exploration of the moral architecture woven into reality.

Future Volumes

Further movements in the unfolding philosophical canon.

A Final Invitation

If this book has spoken to you, consider continuing the

journey through the canon.

Each volume is a threshold — another step toward clarity, coherence, and the quiet center that has always known your name.

THE PILGRIM OF THE INNER DAWN

A VISUAL GUIDE TO THE MYTHIC AND PHILOSOPHICAL WORKS

These works form a single unfolding journey - a canon built to guide the reader from myth to meaning, and from meaning to coherence.

MYTHIC WING — NARRATIVE FOUNDATIONS

PHILOSOPHICAL WING — THE FOUNDATIONAL FRAMEWORK

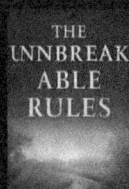

FURIHR VOLUMES IN THE CANON ARE CURRENTLY IN DEVELOPMENT.

www.ingramcontent.com/pod-product-compliance
Lightning Source LLC
Chambersburg PA
CBHW071323080526
44587CB00018B/3331